1

Journey To Mental Health

My Personal Story

by

Mary Beth Smith

Table of Contents

Preface

At some point in their lives everyone has to make a decision: Do I want to become a better person, a person who is kind, compassionate and works for a good cause or do I want to become an evil person: someone who has no compassion or feelings for others and only cares about their need to appear important in the eyes of others—a person who loves only themselves. If the person chooses to become good something can happen—a spiritual experience which makes them see that there is only one choice left to them—they must do only what is right. They can no longer do wrong. At this point they don't know what actions they must take in the future to make the world a better place. There is a lot of work to do before they can know this. Once they know this they will become psychologically healthy—no longer self-absorbed. Their self-esteem will be realistic—they know who they are. No matter how inferior they felt before, they now feel they are needed. They have lost their fears and have become quite calm. They are un-selfconscious, funny, do not care what other people think and are comfortable in their own skins. They know their purpose in life has something to do with helping others.

The healthy person is no longer torn about what

they should do. They will know what to do when given a choice. They must choose compassion and actively pursue behavior that is good.

I mention here good people because I believe a good person can attain psychological health even if they are bipolar. That doesn't mean that they can stop taking their medication. However possibly they may be able to reduce the amount they take (with the help of their psychiatrist).

The ones who are evil choose selfishness, hate, cruelty and greed. They hate and try to destroy those who are good. And the good are clear minded enough to detect the evil in people who have gone down this path.

This begs the question. If we are repelled by a leader who is evil, what leaders should we get behind? Which leaders should we support? I voted for Ohio governor Kasich. I thought he might neutralize Donald Trump. If not now maybe later. But I now would prefer someone better than Kasich. He probably is staying in the public eye to get voted into a better position after he leaves the governorship. There's Marco Rubio who so obviously grabs the limelight while trying desperately to vote the party line. He would have made a great president though with his eloquence and knowledge of foreign policy.

Obama

Obama went to Germany in May of 2017 to receive the German Media Award. Coincidently President Trump was in Europe also.

Obama said:

> If you had to choose a time to be born you'd choose now. Women can vote in every democracy. You have the freedom to choose who you can love. The market economies generate wealth. The world is a more tolerant one because of the work of previous generations. No E.U. country will attack another. But we cannot afford complacency. We need a strong united Europe to uphold the democratic recovery from depression, the Paris Climate Change Agreement, cure Ebola and end extreme poverty. America and Europe need to keep on moving toward a solution to those problems. We need the inspiration to move forward.

> This is a defining moment. The U.S. and the world must ensure women's rights, education for all and ensure the continuance of the rule of law. If we do not support these things people will argue that

we no longer need the freedom of the press.

We need a strong united Europe to uphold democracy, recovery from depression, the Paris Climate Agreement and end Ebola and extreme poverty.

The struggle for human dignity goes on. We have to work together to replace fear with hope.

We have a lot of work to do. We are now at a defining moment.

Conversion

Making the decision to become a better person often happens when a person is suffering so much that they have to reach out to God and ask for help. My grandfather, an agnostic, was in the hospital with encephalomyelitis and pleurisy. Because of the pleurisy—a swelling of the membrane that covers the lungs—he was in constant pain. He said he was "at the end of my rope." In great pain he said, "God, if there is a God, please help me." Suddenly he felt a spiritual presence. He said to his wife, "I want the priest to come." He converted to Catholicism after that.

It's as simple and complicated as that. Simple because the experience is brief and not evident to others. Complicated because the experience may be a factor of spiritual growth over many years. No one knows what causes this except that it occurs more often to those who pray, even if they just pray for a moment like my grandfather.

I'm only writing about spiritual health because it will bring about mental health. If one is bipolar they still have to take medication but perhaps they will be able to take less.

Evil

Judge Not Lest Ye Be Judged!

According to writer M. Scott Peck this doesn't mean to never judge. It means that once you have achieved a certain amount of spiritual maturity you are ready to judge. And you also are clear headed enough to judge others. If a person is good they can detect the truly evil and those on a downhill path. Those on a down hill path have some or all of the seven deadly sins. If a person is guilty of all of the seven deadly sins then there may be no way back for that person.

The seven deadly sins are pride, greed, lust, envy, gluttony, wrath and sloth.

Pride is feeling foolishly important. Pride is refusing to accept help or suggestions from anybody else. It is very dangerous when the person has great power over others.

A few Civil War generals thought the survival of the nation depended on them alone. Yankee General John Buford drove himself so hard that he died within 6 months of the battle of Gettysburg from exhaustion and exposure. General George McClellan was vain. Lincoln said to him, "It is an

9

enormous task." McClellan said, "I can do it all." McClellan was eventually fired. Another symptom of pride is thinking you are better than others—smarter, better looking, richer. This prevents compassion. It causes you to look down on others who have what you think is a mediocre job—a janitor for example.

Greed is the desire for excess wealth. It causes a person to want more than they need and it complicates their life.

Lust is an inordinate desire for sex, food, power or other object.

Envy is the desire for what another person has even if you have no need for that object.

Gluttony is over eating or drinking.

Anger can cause a person to take immediate physical action without any thought.

Sloth has been defined as ignoring the gifts of grace: prophecy, service, teaching, generosity, leading, doing acts of mercy.

I know one person who is very prideful and will not accept psychiatric help even when her anxiety level is almost unbearable. She's also greedy enough to have stolen money from her own relatives.   She sometimes screams in anger for little reason. She is obese but seems to eat and drink alcoholic beverages a great deal. She wants the things that others have even though she owns more than anyone. At one time I was a little manic so I judged that I should do the opposite of what she told me to do. I never went wrong in doing that.

I've make it a point to try to do the opposite of what President Trump seems to want. I needed a new volunteer job but had no idea what I should volunteer for. Then the president threatened to cut Meals on Wheels. Right away I called them and volunteered.   Others people had the same idea. There was a 500 percent increase in volunteer signups and 50 times more online donations than before.

Meals on Wheels gets funding from the *Administration on Aging* and donations. Trump didn't really cut Meals on Wheels but his proposed cuts to other programs bothered people. And the rumor that he was cutting Meals on Wheels angered people. Use your judgement in deciding what to do or not to do. Obey the law. If you are on a path of spiritual growth you will make the right decisions.

I. Manic Depression

I am bipolar. I did not know that until I was 35 and had a manic psychosis. Beginning in my early 20s my moods would go up and down. I thought they were in the normal range. The "up" moods made me daring and energetic. I wasn't afraid of anything—flying, hang gliding, motorcycle riding. The "down" moods made me feel like my head was cloudy but it wasn't incapacitating. During either mood I could do a lot of work.

Bipolar disorder runs in my family. My sister has it, her son had it and his daughter has it. Two first cousins committed suicide. So did my nephew. I think doctors should pay more attention to this part of your family history and warn you about the addictions and possible manic psychosis.

The unfortunate aspect of bipolar disorder at this stage is that you develop addictions—addictions to lift the bad mood. You have no idea that you have a mental illness so, at this point, you won't see a psychiatrist. The addiction will ruin your physical health or your personal life—or both. Some addictions are:

    alcohol
    tobacco

opioids
prescription drugs
cocaine
cannabis
amphetamines
hallucinogens
inhalants
kleptomania
compulsive setting of fires
gambling
food
sex
pornography
working
exercising
cutting behavior
shopping

One woman explained the results of medication on her addictions:

> The adultery stopped. The cyber sex, the phone sex, the stealing, the lying, the cheating, the suicidal ideation, the homicidal ideation, it all came to screeching halt.

My addiction was related to sex. Becoming infatuated with totally inappropriate people—married men for example. I did it to lift my mood. When I got married, my mentally ill husband began to visit a single mother of two—every night —to lift *his* mood. Naturally I developed a crush on someone at work to lift my mood.

My husband was my only friend. I was also under a lot of pressure at work. I expected too much of myself. (Never work yourself to death even if your boss tells you to.) People began teasing me about a woman my husband was seeing at my place of work. She sat right next to him and brought him lunch everyday. He began to go to her house every night, not coming home until 2 A.M. Even his mother said to throw him out.

I couldn't stand it any more. I flew to Maryland to be with my mother. Then I flew back to Florida to face the same situation. I swung into a mania.

Recently a younger man had rejected me. I threw some clothes into a suitcase and drove my VW up a windy road. Suddenly I decided to crash my car into a tree. I thought I would be reincarnated and reunited with the man who had rejected me. I thought, "This will hurt but it will be worth it."

They had to use the jaws of life to cut me out of the car. At the hospital I was given 4 units of blood. Two tubes were put in my right lung. X-rays were done of my chest and back. The x-rays really hurt. Nothing was done for the several broken ribs I had. A screw was put into my broken right ankle.

Because my injuries were on the right side and Christ had a wound on his right side, I thought I was Jesus Christ.

A psychiatrist was called and he gave me an antipsychotic.

I started seeing the psychiatrist who kept me on Haldol for 3 weeks. I begged him to take me off it. It was making me very restless. When he took me off of it I plunged into a deep depression: a flat, numb, pessimistic mood. Reading was impossible. Going to the beach didn't help. Nor did watching TV. My mother and I went to lunch every day and sat in the bright sunlight which helped a little. I had no energy to do anything.

A friend who was an alcoholic described the feeling this way:

> When I stop drinking everything becomes bland. I get no pleasure out of anything. Nothing helps. Not TV. Not food. I just sit there and think, "So what?" Then, when I start to drink again, things go back to normal.

I was relieved to hear that at least one person in the world had the same feelings as I.

The next time I saw the psychiatrist, I correctly

described my feelings.

"Oh, that is just the depression," he said, laughing. He prescribed a mild tranquilizer which could have worsened the depression. (But didn't.)

One day he arranged to meet me outside his office. As soon as we got to the meeting place, we had sex.
I had promised myself to move heaven and earth in order to get help for my condition. Obviously this guy had no intention of helping me. I decided to switch doctors immediately.

When I called the new doctor, Dr. Cross, she was puzzled as to why I would want to switch doctors in midstream. "The doctor and I agreed that it would be better if I saw a woman doctor," I said. Dr. Cross made an appointment to see me.

"Tell me what happened?" she said after giving me a test for depression. I was glad to tell her. No one else had ever asked before. When I told the other doctor about it—elation followed by depression—he made up some latin sounding name for it. He didn't even try to get to the bottom of the problem. (Probably so he could take advantage of me.) I am angry about it to this day.

Dr. Cross had to try a few medications until she found one that worked. And that took weeks. This was in 1985 and the meds were not as fast acting as they are today. Nor could the doctor predict what medication would work best.

Early on I decided to choose an attitude to take towards this chronic illness. On thinking about it I had 2 choices:

(1) Continue to whine and complain.
(2) Act with the courage and dignity my father had when faced with the results of polio.

He always laughed at any humiliating experiences caused by using crutches (such as falls). When something bad happened to him he would make up a funny story about it as it occurred.

I decided to act like my father.

More About Bipolar Disorder

IQ

People with bipolar disorder are born with an above average IQ. But after a psychotic episode their IQ may deteriorate. The verbal part of the IQ remains the same. The nonverbal part which includes picture completion, object assembly and block design can become lower.

Class

Bipolar disorder most often occurs in the upper middle class because of the family's higher IQ and the achievements of the hypomanic family members. Hypomanic people are moody but they are likable, energetic, creative, funny and self confident. They do well in their chosen field.

Weight Gain

Atypical antipsychotics in the short term can cause minor weight gain. With some of the atypical antipsychotics the weight gain doesn't level off. They cause an increase in appetite and people continue to gain weight for several months. The weight gain is of the abdominal type—the most dangerous. That type causes insulin resistance and cardiovascular problems.

Lithium can cause a 5 to 10 percent weight gain. People sometimes stop taking it because of that. It has an effect on carbohydrate metabolism including a mild anti-insulin effect.

Regular exercise, restriction of sugary drinks, avoidance of simple carbohydrates, taking antipsychotics that do not cause uncontrollable weight gain and avoiding some antidepressants will help.

Untreated episodes of manic and hypomania become more frequent and more severe.

Ideally the medication should be taken before a psychotic episode happens.

Manic-Depressive Illnesses and Recurrent Depression

This section is from Kay Redfield Jamison, Touched With Fire, Manic-Depressive Illness and the Artistic Temperament, New York, N.Y. 1993

Frederick K. Goodwin, MD, Kay Redfield Jamison, Ph.D., Manic-Depressive Illness, Bipolar II Disorders and Recurrent Depression, Oxford

19

New York: Oxford University press 2007

Kay Redfield Jamison, <u>An Unquiet Mind</u>, New York: Vintage books, A division of Random House, Inc., 1995

My book <u>Healing Manic Depression and Depression What Works: Based on What Helped Me</u> contains all footnotes for the sections on manic depression.

> My mind was beginning to have to scramble a bit to keep up with itself, as ideas were coming so fast that they intersected one another at every conceivable angle. There was a neuronal pileup on the high-ways of my brain, and the more I tried to slow down my thinking the more I became aware that I couldn't. My enthusiasms were going into overdrive as well, although there often was some underlying thread of logic in what I was doing.—Kay Redfield Jamison, *An Unquiet Mind*

Mania

Common signs of mania and hypomania are as follows:
• elevated mood
• decreased need for sleep
• rapid speech
• fast thinking
• inflated self-esteem
• poor judgement
• risk taking
• spending too much money

Unlike mania, hypomania doesn't affect your ability to function. It can cause excessive involvement in pleasurable but dangerous activities. If followed by depression the depression can be severe and frequent. The mild form of hypomania is quite productive. Unlike hypomania, mania does affect your ability to function and sometimes includes bizarre behavior, grandiose delusions, and/or visual and auditory hallucinations. It can also include elation.

Theodore Roethke said, "I didn't sleep much. I just walked around with this wonderful feeling." Robert Lowell said, "I believed I could stop cars and paralyze their forces by merely standing in the middle of the highway with my arms outspread...."

The aftermath of mania is usually depression. Before lithium, fully 1/5 of manic-depressives died by suicide. Today 1/4 to 1/2 of patients have attempted suicide at least once.

Depression

The most common symptom of depression is diminished interest or pleasure in all or almost all activities.

Other signs are:
• changes in appetite
• changes in sleep patterns
• loss of motivation
• feelings of guilt
• inability to concentrate
• slowing of speech, thought and movement
• recurring thoughts of death or suicide

French composer Hector Berlioz wrote, "One's only wish is for silence, solitude and the oblivion of sleep...nothing has meaning...."

Austrian composer Hugo Wolf wrote, "I would like most to hang myself on the nearest branch of the cherry trees standing now in full bloom." F. Scott Fitzgerald wrote, "Every act of life from the morning toothbrush to the friend at dinner had become an effort...." Poet Edward Thomas wrote,

22

"I am weary of everything. I stay because I am too weak to go."

Bipolar I, bipolar II and recurrent depression are included by some scientists in manic-depressive illness. Recurrent means that the major depression occurred more than once. Abraham Lincoln had at least 2 major depressions. One when he was found lying on the grave of his first love in the rain and the other when he broke up with his fiance Mary Todd. His friends had to hide all sharp objects from him after the breakup.

Cyclothymia

Cyclothymia is the mildest form of manic-depressive illness. It consists of alternating moods of hypomania and depression. It usually starts in adolescence or early adulthood. The patient may go on to develop bipolar I.

Bipolar I

Bipolar I is the most severe form of the illness. An episode can begin with hyperactivity. The person usually then becomes agitated, paranoid and shows signs of grandiosity. Fifty percent become unable to distinguish reality from fantasy.

Bipolar II

Bipolar II is hypomania alternating with periods of depression. Many people go undiagnosed because they only seek help for the depression. It impairs the person's functioning at work and at home. It is not considered bipolar II if the symptoms are brought on by an antidepressant or other medications.

Bipolar NOS

Bipolar NOS (not otherwise specified) does not meet any other criteria. It may not last long enough; it may be a hypomanic episode without depressive symptoms; it may be caused by a medication or underlying health condition; it may be superimposed on another disorder.

Mixed Mania

Mixed mania is where both mania and depression occur simultaneously, or alternate frequently during the day.

Postpartum Depression and Psychosis

Only 1 in 1,000 women get postpartum psychosis or depression. Without treatment it lasts for months. It is thought to be related to manic-depressive illness because the symptoms are almost identical.

Bipolar women are at high risk of getting it (50-75 percent). They are treated with lithium before the birth and lithium or other mood stabilizers afterwards. Since sleep disruptions cause mania, they should not be allowed to care for their infant during the first 6 weeks after birth.

Twenty-five percent of bipolar women had their bipolar disorder triggered by postpartum psychosis. Woman who have already had postpartum problems have a 50 percent chance of having it again at future births. While the woman is in the later stages of pregnancy, lithium is given because it is much less likely to harm the fetus than the other mood stabilizers valproate and carbamazepine.

Andrea Yates was known to have problems with postpartum psychosis. Her husband was told to never leave her alone. He left her alone for 1 hour and she methodically drowned each of her 5 children. She called 911 and said, "I just killed my kids."

In her first trial she was found guilty. The verdict was overturned on appeal, and in her second trial she was declared not guilty by reason of insanity. She now has been diagnosed with bipolar disorder and lives in a State Hospital where she is given some freedom. Her lawyer hopes she will be freed soon. He is now dedicated to educating the public about women's mental health problems.

Shelley Ash had never heard of postpartum psychosis when she became pregnant. She got it "out of the blue." When she found herself with an urge to kill the baby, she ran to the bathroom and took an overdose of pain killers. She survived and has since devoted her time to spreading information about the illness.

After having a baby, Melanie Stokes was so depressed that she could no longer eat, drink or swallow. She started to dream up ways of killing herself. She was put in the hospital several times. One time after she got out of the hospital she jumped out of a 12 story window, killing herself. Her parents are now trying to inform the public about this illness.

Stress

Manic-depressive illness is first triggered by some major life stress. Life events that trigger the illness include losing a loved one, changing jobs, and moving. It only happens if the person has inherited a genetic vulnerability to the illness. Just over 1 percent of people have some form of the illness. One person in 20 will have a major depression over their lifetime. Patients find subsequent episodes harder to explain.

26

If manic-depression and recurrent depression are not treated properly they will occur more often and worsen over time.

Genetics

Bipolar disorder and recurrent depression run in families due to a genetic vulnerability. It may require 3 or more such genes to produce a vulnerability. The individual carrying the genes may never get the illness but they may pass it on to their children. If an identical twin has bipolar disorder the likelihood of the other twin having it is 70 to 100 percent. In fraternal twins it is 20 percent. If one parent has manic-depression the likelihood of their child getting it is 28 percent. If one parent is bipolar and the other has a mood disorder the likelihood is 75 percent.

Creativity

Healthy writers are more productive when they are hypomanic. Bipolar or unipolar writers do better when they are in a normal mood.

People with mood disorders are gifted in many ways and their siblings are more likely to be gifted also. IQ does not seem to relate very much to creativity. The great creative genius in physics, Richard Feynman, only had an IQ in the low 120's.

27

A disproportionate number of great writers and artists have suffered from bipolar spectrum disorders and under some circumstances, creativity can be facilitated by such disorders.

One study examined eminent poets, writers and artists. The poets were 50 percent more likely than the general public to have been treated for a mood disorder. Biographers were the least likely to suffer from such disorders.

The list below shows some poets and their symptoms:

• Samuel Johnson—severe recurrent melancholia
• William Blake—hallucinations
• Robert Burns—severe recurrent melancholia
• William Wordsworth—moody and violent temper
• Sir Walter Scott—melancholy
• Samuel Taylor Coleridge—despair, grandiose and agitated
• Robert Southey—unduly excitable
• George Gordon, Lord Byron—recurrent melancholia, rage
• John Clare—25 years in an insane asylum, hallucinations
• John Keats—periods of depression followed by periods of intense activity and exhilaration

Medication

There is no cure for bipolar disorder. Bipolar disorder is a life-long mental health disorder that can be treated well with certain medications, but it will never go away. Fortunately there are a lot of good drugs out there to treat bipolar, and if you work with a psychiatrist who can help you find the right dose of the right drug you can lead a relatively normal life with few interruptions from your disease. Doctors now agree that it is malpractice to treat depressive and manic-depressive illness without medication.

Mania and hypomania are treated with mood stabilizers. These can cause tremor, weight gain, cognitive dulling and bad memory.

Untreated, episodes become more frequent and more severe.

Depression is treated with anti-depressants and it is important to continue the medication to prevent recurring depression.

The side effects of anti-depressants may be drowsiness, sedation, headaches and tension. If the side effects become too difficult to handle, the patient can be switched to another medication. Interestingly, lithium maintenance has been shown to lower the risk of suicide.

II. Mystical Experiences

This part was influenced by <u>'Pass It On' The Story of Bill Wilson and how the A.A. message reached the world</u>, Alcoholics Anonymous World Services, Inc., New York, N.Y.: 1984.

<u>Alcoholics Anonymous Comes of Age: A Brief History of A.A.</u>, Alcoholics Anonymous World Services, Inc., New York: 1957, 1985

<u>Alcoholics Anonymous, The Story of How Many Thousands of Men and Women Have Recovered from Alcoholism</u>, third edition, New York: Alcoholics Anonymous World Services, Inc. 1976.

Mary Beth Smith, <u>The Joy of Life: A Biography of Theodore Roosevelt</u>, amazon.com

A friend of the founders of A.A. had been to Carl Jung. He asked Dr. Jung to cure him of alcoholism. Dr. Jung said there was no medical or psychiatric cure for alcoholism. The patient asked him if there was anything else that might help him. Jung replied, "There is provided you could become the subject of a spiritual or religious experience— in short, a genuine conversion." He said that such experiences were relatively rare. He said, "Place yourself in a religious atmosphere and hope for the best." He joined a religious group and did have a conversion experience and stopped drinking as a result.

Dr. Harry Tiebout, a psychiatrist who was in on the beginning of Alcoholics Anonymous, had a very difficult patient. She had a "hard narcissistic egocentric core."

The patient joined A.A. and accepted the existence of a higher power.

Little by little she changed. No longer was she so defensive, aggressive and suspicious. She now looked peaceful. The lines in her face had softened and she looked kind.

She had had a religious experience. A.A. believes the alcoholic has to become totally humble before the religious experience can happen. The person has to let go of their pride before they can ask for outside help. Once Dr. Tiebout's patient got rid of her narcissism she was ready to accept his help.

Bill Wilson, one of the founders of A.A., was in the hospital to get help for his alcoholism. When the alcohol wore off he fell into a very bad depression. He thought there was nothing left for him but death or madness. He was at what he called the "jumping-off place." He was an atheist but he prayed, "If there be a God, let him show Himself!" Suddenly is he saw a white light, a

mountain and felt a wind "not of air, but of spirit."
This, he felt, must be God. He felt ecstasy and
remained in that state for some time.

I was writing a book about Theodore Roosevelt. I
was writing about his Rough Riders who fought in
the Spanish American war. I was trying to
understand the connection he felt with the Rough
Riders. They were a mixed group of people:

A 37-year-old sheriff from New Mexico
cowboys from Arizona
full and mixed breed Indians
50 or so Ivy Leaguers
Bucky O'Neil, a famous sheriff and the mayor of
Prescott
Captain Llewellen of New Mexico who was a
noted peace officer
Pollock, a full blooded Pawnee
Captain Maximillan Luna from New Mexico who
was the only man of pure Spanish blood
Texas Rangers
Buffalo Soldiers who were black men who fought
as bravely as any of them.

He said of the regiment:

> I can hardly say how proud I am of this
> regiment. It is so typically American! It is
> just the ideal body for me to lead; and the
> men are devoted to me, and in the field I

can lead and handle them as I think no other man could. Easterners and Westerners alike do even more than their duty.

All—easterners and westerners, northerners and southerners, officers and men, cowboys and college graduates, wherever they came from and whatever their social position—possessed in common the traits of hardihood and a thirst for adventure. They were to a man born adventurers, in the old sense of the word....

More than ever, I fail to get the relations of this regiment and the universe straight.

I tried to understand the connection he felt to this group of soldiers. I had not felt anything like it myself. He probably had an epiphany at this time that he was to become a great leader of the American people. I wanted to understand the connection with the soldiers.

I was volunteering in the hospital gift shop when I had a mystical experience. Several of the volunteers were standing around talking. I thought, "This is a group of very good women and I am a part of that." Suddenly I felt as if I was floating. I looked down. I was still firmly planted in my chair. The feeling was wonderful—like a spirit must feel when released from it's earthly body. I noticed I didn't feel the normal itchiness in my skin. It was something like floating in a warm ocean. It didn't last long. In seconds I was back in my chair with the normal aches and pains everyone has.

The next time it happened was at my 30th class reunion. I noticed how all the women were still good looking and, based on their jobs, very intelligent. I thought about how they were all alike in this way. Once again I felt as if I was floating. It didn't last long. I was glad I wasn't actually floating because that would have been embarrassing. That was the last time I had that experience. Since then I have been much calmer and more self-confident.

Mania

Since that experience I have not had depression or anxiety but I have experienced manias. One mania began when a published author emailed me that my book on Theodore Roosevelt was an excellent introduction to the man. I was so excited by this that I became manic and wrote nonsensical things to the Theodore Roosevelt Association e-group, a group set up to report hard facts—when and where was the next meeting to be held for example. They e-mailed me, "Stop talking, Mrs. Smith!" That brought me down a little. It wasn't over but I realized what was happening.

Another time I tried to organize the papers in my desk. I also thought I knew when an actor had died—the exact time and day, and knew when an in-law had died—exact time and day. Finally I asked to be admitted to the hospital. I told the doctor I was thinking about suicide. (Who doesn't think about suicide?) The nurses watched me like a hawk. I did guess correctly about the dates and times of those deaths. The in-law appeared to me in what I thought was a dream. She was dressed in a beautiful gown and a feeling of love was emanating from her. I thought that was odd because my dreams of love are about men not old ladies. It was a strong feeling of love.

When I got back from the hospital I saw that I had
thrown my papers all over the room.
Lately I've had manias where the computer "talks"
to me. It will say, "Who do you think should run
for president?" I'll type in a name. Then the
computer will say, "Don't type his name. The
government is watching."

I was driven into a mania by listening to a speech
by Governor Kasich after he won the New
Hampshire primary. I parsed the speech trying to
figure out what he meant. I decided it meant I
should go to Illinois to a sub shop with the same
name as a phrase in his speech. I decided to take a
bus there and vote in the Illinois primary. I didn't
do that though.

Later I was listening to music as the lyrics
appeared on the screen. Suddenly the words
"GOD IS GREAT" appeared on the screen. Those
words weren't there. Then I said, "I want to see
my dead father." It showed a baby. I thought,
"There is reincarnation. My father would be
reincarnated as a baby by now." I became more
and more manic. I began yelling and screaming at
my husband. My husband called my doctor and
he said call an ambulance. "You can't drive her
because she may try to jump out of the car." The
hospital didn't have room for another psychiatric
patient so I was taken to a hospital for physically
ill people. While there I threw away two valuable

36

rings because they had belonged to distant relatives I didn't care for. I really regret that now.

I was taken to a psychiatric unit later and stayed only a few days. I was heavily medicated and when I got out, my hands began to shake. The doctor took me off the extra meds but the shaking hasn't stopped. Now I take meds for the shaking which allow me to type.

Books

In 2013 I was told I could cheaply self publish my book on Theodore Roosevelt. After that I researched and wrote 7 more books. I enjoy doing that but know that others need to find hobbies that they are suited for. Writing nonfiction is not going to help anybody (except me). No one reads my self published books since I don't have a way of advertising them. I read several books on each subject, then write it out like a giant term paper. I feel it is important to understand certain presidents —the great ones. Someone once said if you want to understand yourself, study Lincoln. I did that and do better understand myself. Now I'm studying Dwight D. Eisenhower, Supreme Commander of the Allied Forces. He wrote a clear and logical book about his part in World War II which is a huge help to me at this stage. Later I'll write about his presidency.

Following is a list of the five greatest presidents:

Lincoln
Washington
F.D.R.
Theodore Roosevelt
Dwight D. Eisenhower.

I want to learn how these men became great. Most

started quite young to learn what they needed to know to be a success later in life.

Sociopaths

I include this section because good and evil is mentioned in the preface to this book. Any patient seeking help for mental health problems is not a sociopath. Sociopaths are perfectly happy with their lives even if they've committed rape or murder. They never feel uncomfortable or ashamed enough to feel the need for a psychiatrist or a psychologist.

Sociopaths are aggressive, cunning, manipulative and have the ability to appear benevolent. They can be superficially charming in order to hide selfish motives. They blame others for the results of their own conduct. They lie. They can't feel normal human emotions like empathy. They are certain they will never have to pay for their criminal behavior.

Famous sociopaths include:

Adolf Hitler
Charles Manson
John Wayne Gacy
Jim Jones
Ted Bundy
David Koresh
Scott Peterson

There are many others who don't commit murder but they ruin people's lives. About 1 out of 100 people are sociopaths.

*****

I've read that God is love and God helps individuals grow spiritually. But God needs the help of good people to make the world a better place. God needs *bodies*. God helps people develop spiritually so that they will be ready to help when they are needed. Some of my heroes Lincoln, Frederick Douglass, Dwight D. Eisenhower, and Theodore Roosevelt made a decision early in their lives to do the best at every job they were given. As a child Theodore Roosevelt (1901-1909) read about every country in the world. He also toured Europe as a child. By the time he was president he understood each country's unique qualities. He feared the warmongering of the Germans, predicted the coming bloody revolution of Russia and knew the necessity of being respectful to the Japanese who, he predicted, might become warlike if offended. His autobiography explains why he did the things he did. For example he sent a huge fleet of ships around the world to impress the Germans and the Japanese, possible future enemies of the United States.

41

Lincoln learned to read as a child, rebelling against his father who wanted him to become a farmer like everybody else. When he left his family at the age of 21 he was able to obtain books that taught him grammar, the law, science, math and other subjects. Free from his father he studied and read all the time. He served 4 terms in the state legislature. Then he became an excellent lawyer although he felt called to some higher purpose than that. He also made it a point to practice giving speeches saying that people prefer to hire lawyers who they have heard speak. He also studied what the Founders said so that when he came back into the public eye, he was able to prove that they had expected slavery to die out. He was invited to give a speech in New York and later in other northern states. He was so eloquent that he became very well known and became president.

Lincoln, Robert E. Lee, Eisenhower and TR were not saints as children. Lincoln was trying to lift his depression by reading. Many children begin their personal development by doing what their parents ask. Lyndon Johnson was rarely complimented by his mother for getting good grades. She complimented him just often enough that he worked very hard on his school work. One little girl Anne de Guigné had a spiritual experience at age 4 which changed her from a holy terror who rubbed sand in her baby brother's eyes to a child who became devoted to her mother who had just been widowed. She became such a good child that after she died at age 11 the Catholic Church named her "Venerable." Venerable means servant of God. It is rare for a child to be named venerable but all who knew her attested to her goodness. Needless to say most people don't become that spiritually advanced until they are middle-aged or older (if at all).

III. My Up and Down Life

1. Two Years Old

I can remember being 2-years-old probably because I was in an automobile accident at that time. I don't remember the accident but I remember the aftermath. We had emerged from the car and were walking to a house. Everyone was talking at the same time but I remember my sister saying AMBULANCE. I had hit my nose on the dashboard of the car and my father was worried it was broken. I was scared and crying.

We went into a split level house and down into a sunken living room. I sat on the sofa and looked for a TV. The owner didn't have one—this was 1951 and many people waited until years later to buy one. Then I noticed a tall radio from the 1920s. I felt comforted because we had one in our cellar.

My father decided to drive me to the hospital. On the way I noticed lights on poles, shinning brightly, illuminating the street. I remember thinking, "I should know what they are. Why have I never noticed them before?"

When we got to the hospital we faced a number of

steps at the entryway. My father said, "You go first." My father had lost the use of his legs in the polio epidemic of 1944. After I got to the top of the stairs he climbed them using his crutches and braces as he had practiced in therapy.

Someone sat me on a table. Two or three men dressed all in white came in and shone a light into my nostrils. My nose was quite alright so we were allowed to leave.

I have other memories of being 2 years old. They mostly were of that Christmas. My sisters sat my brother in a little fire engine he had gotten for Christmas. They told me to stand next to him. That made me very angry. They were always posing me and taking pictures. They were much older than I, 14 and 16, and when they laughed at something I said I thought they were ridiculing me. In the picture I am almost hidden by the Christmas tree and I look annoyed. The baby pooped in the little car. I had already been toilet trained by that time. I remember thinking he was very stupid. From then on I would make a mental note of every stupid thing he did or said. He was just 9 months of age and naturally was not toilet trained.

Once he could walk my mother showered all of her attention on him. I began to have trouble eating an entire meal. I could only eat about 2 spoonfuls of what was placed before me so my mother heated up milk for me at dinner time. I probably wanted to retreat to babyhood. I also wet my bed until I was 6.

I tried to hurt my brother. One time I slammed the lid of a secretary desk on his hand which actually help straighten out one of his thumbs. (He had an operation later to correct his bent thumbs.) Another time I was walking toward the end of the upstairs hall when I noticed my brother standing there. A voice in my head said, "Push him down," which I did but my mother saw it and said, "Don't hurt your brother." After that, I only verbally abused him. I did that until I moved out of the house at 25 years of age.

My brother and I used to watch television every morning. When I was five years old my mother appeared at the door with Uncle Jimmy and said, "Uncle Jimmy is taking me to the hospital to get the baby." We didn't understand that babies came out of the mother's body. We just said, "okay."

My sisters watched us for a couple of days. Then they drove us to Mercy Hospital to get my mother and the baby. On the way I had a panic attack and from then on had frequent ones especially if an adult who was not my parent was driving us to school. I also had them at parochial school when walking in a line down the aisle of the church. I knew if I ran away or fell down from the attack it would be very embarrassing so I feared both the panic attack and the embarrassing aftermath of one. Some people who attend mass on Sundays sit on the pew nearest the door so they can easily escape if they have an attack. As an adult I had them while landing an airplane, but only if my instructor was there.   Alone, I had no trouble landing a plane. Panic attacks consist of two parts. The first part is the actual attack. The second part is the fear that you will make a fool of yourself running away or collapsing on the ground. That part of the attack lasts much longer. One should let the first part of the attack come and go and remind yourself that your thoughts are causing the second part of the attack. I say this "litany against fear" from the novel *Dune* by Frank Herbert while I'm having the attack:

> I must not fear.
> Fear is the mind-killer.
> Fear is the little-death that brings total
> obliteration.
> I will face my fear.
> I will permit it to pass over me and through
> me.
> And when it has gone past I will turn the
> inner eye to see its path.
> Where the fear has gone there will be
> nothing. Only I will remain.

I had panic attacks many mornings during the car

pool rides to school when my mother was not driving.

2. Kindergarten

The entire year of kindergarten was frightening. The teacher was sarcastic. Once I asked what color to make the sail of a sail boat. She said, "Brown." After seeing that I had painted it brown she grabbed it and took it away. At lunch time when she saw I couldn't finish my sandwich she had all the kids surround me and say, "Hurry up, Mary Beth. Hurry up." I told my mother about this and she began to give me only a quarter of a sandwich. That satisfied my teacher but she recorded me as being retarded.

On my first day of kindergarten I noticed that the children, girls especially, were very talkative. Right then I knew I was different. I didn't feel drawn to pick out a friend like the others did. I couldn't think of anything to say. Throughout my school years I had but two friends—one school friend and one neighborhood friend. I had no idea of what to say to other children.

Sometimes, to get us to behave, the teacher would tell us that if we didn't quiet down a truck would come and take us to the "dog and cat school." I didn't have a pet and I thought dogs and cats would be taken with us in the truck. She would leave the room and we would all begin to cry. Then she'd come back saying she was giving us another chance.

Even as an adult I was able to form the thoughts I wanted to say but it was as if I was unable to speak them except with my very best friends. Later I would realize that I would always be a quiet person and later still I would become so calm and relaxed that, after listening closely to a person, I would know the best way to respond to him. But that was much later.

3. First Grade – Age 6

My sisters always had their noses in a book, usually a thick text book. I figured that if I wanted to be a big girl I had to imitate their actions. I admired and tried to imitate Sue's artistic talent and Anne's ability to play the piano. Later I took drawing classes and piano lessons. For now, at age 6, I would concentrate on learning to read.

The first day of school the teachers gave me an IQ test. They were expecting me to do poorly because they had been told I was retarded. I hurriedly took the test. It was easy. It showed my IQ to be well above normal (probably 120). "You're smart!" they exclaimed. I felt really good about myself. I began to eat better and I stopped wetting my bed. At about this time my oldest sister got pregnant and moved out of the house. I moved into my sisters' room which my mother said must have made me feel like a big girl. I inherited all their dolls and books. I read the books, when I got older, during the summer.

The first grade classroom was divided into two parts. One part for one teacher. One for another teacher. The second classroom contained advanced books which I took home and tried to read. My mother helped with the difficult words. "Sound it out," she would say. She began to take me to the children's section of the library and tell me to take out all the books I wanted. (I decided more than 5 books would look greedy. I would stick to 5.)

I went to this school for kindergarten, first, second and third grade. It was a private Catholic school with excellent teachers. My brother went for 2 years. My father decided to remove us from that great school and put us in a much inferior Catholic parochial school. I suspect he was trying to save money. That school was overcrowded with baby boomers. The classrooms held 60 to70 pupils and each grade filled 3 classrooms. The teachers were terrible. They wouldn't teach. Instead the children were asked to take turns reading a paragraph from a text book. I think they were not trained to teach. At that time teachers didn't have to have a college education.

The teachers could also be violent. They'd take a ruler and rap a child's knuckles. One threw a boy down the stairs. Occasionally they were sarcastic.

I asked my mother over and over to send me back to the private school. Finally she agreed. She wanted me to attend 8th grade there which would increase the chances I'd get into the high school. It was a good thing she did that because the 8th grade teacher went over and over the questions that would be on the entrance exam. She spent a lot of time on grammar, a subject I found fascinating. We practiced math and other subjects which didn't come naturally to me. She put me in the "after school group" which consisted of all the boys and 5 of us girls who had a chance of winning a scholarship.

4. Grade School

Fourth, fifth, sixth and seventh grades were the most difficult ones for me. I was unpopular. No one noticed me. It was as if I was invisible. One girl decided to make friends with me. She was in a different classroom and thus did not know how unpopular I was. (Remember I said there were three classrooms for every grade.) She was in the same grade, different classroom. She lived in a tiny house while I lived in a tall attractive red brick house. But because I had so little money of my own she had to lend me some. Her father would take us to the public swimming pool which was dirty. Not like the pool my family belonged to which was kept clean. I looked down on her because her pool was dirty and her house so small. I also judged that she was too thin. Even though my brothers and I didn't eat much we still looked healthy. She had shadows around her eyes along with being skeletal looking. She had two cats whose litter box was in the basement. Her house smelled.

I don't judge how people live now but kids tend to compare their lives to other children's. She did not live quite as well as we did even though our needs for food and clothing were not being met. (I will explain why later.)

My best friend was my cousin who I saw on holidays and a younger child who lived next door. The younger child went to a very expensive private school. Her reading level was almost as high as mine and we would spend half our time reading books. The rest of the time was spent playing dress-up with my sister's long abandoned evening gowns. Both my sisters had married early and luckily for me had abandoned their books, dolls and dressy clothing.

After school, if we were lucky we would go to a wealthy girl's house. (Wealthy people lived in big houses and served cokes instead of pepsi, cake instead of toast and jelly.) After eating the cake we would watch TV in the basement. If less lucky we would go to the slightly poorer child's house and pig out on toast and jelly.

At the poorer child's house I often wondered where the books were. One of the previous owners was one of the rare women doctors allowed to practice medicine in the area. After studying in Holland she came to New York and then to Hopkins in Baltimore to re-study everything she had already learned in Holland. The fact that most men were in the service during the war gave women the opportunity to study and practice medicine. Her family had left Holland to live in New York in the 1940s because they were Jewish sympathizers. She became a pediatrician. Her name was difficult

55

to pronounce so the children called her Dr. Annie. Our pediatrician was a man that my sisters had gone to.

Even at 3 or 4-years-old I was impressed with the great number of books she had on shelves in the hallway. No one who has lived there since has had so many books. It looked like many of them were textbooks. Heavy big books.

My mother would take me there because there was a little boy there almost my age. That didn't make me any more sociable a creature because the boy simply stared at me and me at him.

Once my parents said, "Do you want to see the baby?" The girl who would become my close friend was a baby. Her parents were building a house next door. I looked at her with little interest. I didn't know how entertaining she would be in the years to come.

5. 10 Years Old—Wendy Smothered

"One man prays: 'How I may not lose my little child', but you must pray: 'How I may not be afraid to lose him'." - Marcus Aurelius

I went to a parochial school for 4 years. My father would drive my brother and I to school in the morning. In the afternoon the bus would drop us off at the house behind ours rather than drive the extra mile on the windy narrow road to our house.

On April 7, 1960 my brother was in the hospital for a minor operation. (He was having his crooked thumbs straightened.) So I walked alone through the neighbor's yard. I crossed through their yard to our empty lot which we called "the field." I had almost reached the field when I saw my 22-year-old sister carrying her 2 boys one under each arm.

I remember thinking how funny she looked. One boy was under one arm. The other under the other arm. I was about to remark on this when she set the children down, came up to me and said, "Wendy smothered." (her five month old baby.) I began to cry and say, "No... No... No." Then I said, "Is she dead?" She said yes. I asked where she was. "At the funeral home," she said.

She walked me to the house which was filled with

adults.   Even my father had come home from work. I was still crying. (The death had occurred in our house.) She sat me down at the end of the sofa. My mother said, "Does she know....Give her a coke." I finished my coke then went outside and said several times, very dramatically, "It was the only girl." (I had 4 nephews.)

Then I went next door to a friend's house to get some cookies that had been promised me. (Children can compartmentalize). Once I ate those I went to another friend's house. She described the undertaker to me. He was fat and carrying a box under his arm. His fanny wiggled.

Later I asked my mother how Wendy died. She became angry and yelled, "I don't know." My sister had given an explanation to a journalist over the phone. It was a rather involved explanation.

My parent's arranged and paid for the funeral. I heard them attempting to write a death notice. "Unexpectedly," my mother said. "Suddenly," my father said. They went with "suddenly."

The next day my parents and I read the article about the baby's death:

April 8

INFANT STRANGLES TO DEATH IN

BED

> A local infant strangled to death yesterday after she caught her head between the mattress and the footboard of her bed....
>
> Her mother said she found her 5-month-old daughter, Wendy Sue, at 12:30 P.M. She had put her in the bed at 9:30 yesterday.

She died on Thursday. I went with my mother to buy a gown for the baby on Friday. Saturday evening we went to my niece's viewing. I approached the coffin. She looked like a little wax doll. I touched her hand. It was cold. I began to cry. On Sunday my mother drove me to the funeral and afterwards to the cemetery. As my mother and I watched men dig a hole, my cousin, who was standing near me, said to her mother, "I wish I was in that little white box." Her mother said, "You just want people to feel sorry for you." She said, "Yes." I didn't understand. Why would someone want to be in a box they were too big for? (She had a difficult childhood. She wanted sympathy for that.) After the men put the coffin in the ground they shoveled dirt on it. I began to cry and my mother took me to the car.

The night after she died I got what felt like a lump in my throat. Years later I told my therapist. She didn't understand. But it's a common theme in literature that grief makes you feel like you have a lump in your throat. And I certainly did.

Recently my sister told me a little more about the death. After she found her baby dead she ran next door and got our next door neighbor who was dressed in a robe. The neighbor said, "Are you sure she is dead?" She said, "Yes." The neighbor said, "I'll get dressed and will be right over." My sister went back to our house. The neighbor threw on some clothes and came over. "Give her artificial respiration," she said. My sister said, "Why? She's dead." "Do it anyway," she said. She did it. Then the neighbor called the hospital where my brother was having an operation. When my mother answered the phone, She said, "The baby strangled."

My mother worked to take the blame off my sister. She had noticed a wet spot at the end of the mattress which was where the baby smothered. She said maybe it was vomit. She also believed that my sister's mouth smelled like vomit which "proved" she had given artificial respiration. My mother felt guilty because she had decided to put the larger child in the crib instead of the baby.

60

6. My Father

From the reputation and remembrance of my father I learned modesty and a manly character—<u>Meditations,</u> Marcus Aurelius

My father contracted polio when he was at the advanced age of 35. It usually happened to younger people although the victims were increasing in age. (At first it was contracted by toddlers, then by 8 year olds and later by teenagers and 20-somethings.) But my father made the mistake of being active while coming down with the disease. He ran, hiked, swam, and rode horses even when he was coming down with what felt like the flu—his legs hurt awfully he said.

My father was able to counsel the much younger men who were in the hospital with him because of his life experiences. He explained they would be able to go to college because polio hadn't affected their brains. They would be able to get married and have children because only their motor nerves had been affected not their sensory.

When he got home he wanted to go back to work but his job depended on him being able to drive. A wheel-chair-bound friend helped him fasten rods to the clutch and the brake so that they could be worked by hand. Dad was able to

61

use the accelerator since his right foot was okay. He was able to go back to work.

He soon felt a calling to join the National Foundation For Infantile Paralysis (NFIP). He gave speeches about how the NFIP had helped him. They had gotten him into the best hospital for Infantile Paralysis and now he was living a normal life. Later he held leadership positions in the local chapter of the NFIP.

By the time I was born 5 years later I took his paralysis for granted. I barely noticed his braces and crutches. For all I knew other fathers needed assistance walking. I was not exposed to other fathers until I was older. But as a toddler I thought nothing of watching him pull himself up the stairs in a sitting position. Or stopping to grab his crutches as he went down the stairs.

Every Sunday while my mother was at church my father would sit on the edge of the bed and my brother would sit on one of his knees and I would sit on the other as my father showed us the funny papers. Then he would drag himself to the bathroom and fill the tub and we would get into the tub with him.

As long as I knew my father, he never complained about his useless legs. He couldn't walk far on crutches. He had to get permission to park close to

restaurants, his place of work and the Baltimore
Port Authority.

From him I got the feeling that self pity was wrong
especially since what he was putting up with was
so much worse than whatever my problems were.

When I was about 4 we stopped taking baths with
him. When I was 6 he told us we were too big to
sit on his lap.

7. Stoicism

*Stoicism—the endurance of pain or hardship
without a display of feeling and without complaint.*

I have noticed that many great and good people
suffered from hunger or poverty or unhappiness as
children. Eisenhower was poor. Lincoln was poor
and physically abused. Robert E. Lee was poor
and had been abandoned by his father.
Eisenhower, Lincoln and Robert E. Lee
experienced severe depression.

There was really no reason for me to suffer from
hunger as a child, but I did. All three of us
younger siblings did. My passive aggressive
mother was trying to punish my father for yelling
at her for spending too much money. She didn't
cook enough food for the family. My father
always ate a big meal at lunch so when he came
home he was not as hungry as we were. For
breakfast we would eat a cold, one egg omelet.
Lunch consisted of a slice of sandwich meat
between two pieces of white bread. Dinner was
skimpy—a slice of meat, potatoes and a small
amount of vegetables. We were never satisfied
with that especially after having had such a small
breakfast and lunch. My brothers and I noticed
that during the summer and on weekends the
neighborhood children were served filling and

delicious lunches.

In order to save money my mother would buy herself and us inexpensive clothing. But she accessorized her clothing beautifully and looked better than anyone else her age. Not only was our clothing inexpensive, she allowed us to outgrow it. Occasionally that was embarrassing. I had long legs. My slacks would become too short and tight. None of the other kids noticed it but it made me feel self conscious. (Luckily I wore a uniform at school from age 5 to age 17.)

Another difficulty for me was sleeping in a very cold room during the winter. I told my parents how cold it was but they didn't believe me. I was sleeping in the attic. The hot water only got to the attic through a very thin pipe. Years later a workman said, "I hope no one had to sleep up here. It would have been very cold during the winter." I buried myself under piles of blankets and to this day sleep in a room as cold as I can get it. I still pile a lot of covers on myself. (My husband thinks I'm trying to kill myself by burying my head under the covers.)

We suffered unnecessary pain at the dentist. My parents didn't want to pay for the dentist the other neighborhood children had. So we went to the inexpensive dentist who didn't use novocaine. As he drilled a tooth without anything to cut the pain, I would focus on the tree outside his window and try to guide my spirit into that tree.   He probably knew about novocaine but maybe he thought it was a waste of time. An adult would have set him straight on this but he specialized in pediatric dentistry. After watching him yank my little brother's two front teeth with evident enjoyment my mother stopped sending us to any dentist at all until I was 18 and my brothers were 16 and 13.

From watching my father uncomplainingly put up with useless legs I learned that I shouldn't complain. It didn't seem fair that someone still only middle aged could not walk. Just make the best of things. (I assumed the dentist knew what he was doing and I put up with the cold in my bedroom because no one had believed me.) I understand now that you should report anyone who is treating you badly. Because no one believed me when I did report a doctor for molesting me, I never reported such a thing again, although I should have. My father knew when and how to show his anger but was angry so rarely that I didn't pick up on the practice.

Anyway complaining rarely does any good unless you have to stand up and defend your rights.

My father died in 1982. For several years I didn't think much about him. Around 1989 I began trying to understand him better. I wrote several booklets about him and sent them to his other children. But in 2017 I became a little manic and began to make connections between 2 books I was reading—*Seeds of Contemplation* by Thomas Merton and *Merton as I Knew Him*—and my father. One book contained an explanation of the vow of silence that monks take. It said they never say anything unless it is important or helpful. That was just the way my father was. That's why he was so quiet. And that's why we listened when he talked.

When he saw me crying about my 3 gray hairs when I was 19, he explained that it would take 20 years to become totally gray and it would happen gradually. When he saw me crying because my mother said that I was too quiet he told me his mother was quiet and one of his friends said she was the best woman he ever knew *because* she was quiet.. He told each of us to always tell the truth and because he was quiet we listened. He also told us to work hard and earn our own money because he was not going to support us when we grew up.

 When he felt he had to be entertaining, he told funny stories. Otherwise he only spoke if he had something important to say or something helpful, just like the monks. So he seemed to have taken their vow of silence. At some point in his life, probably while recovering from polio, he must have recognized the waste of time idle chatter can be. After he had polio he

67

became efficient in other ways also. For example, he always wrote appointments and other important information, in big bold letters, in a tiny notebook that he kept in the pocket of his jacket. That book never strayed from his pocket. He kept his keys in the same place so he could always find them and told me "a place for everything and everything in its place." He paid his bills on the same day and time every month. He ate breakfast, lunch and dinner at the same time every day and his meals were pretty much the same.

8. Flying

I remarked earlier that people with bipolar disorder take up thrilling and dangerous hobbies. For me flying was not one of them. I decided to learn to fly long before I had symptoms of mania. I made the decision when I read an annual report from Cessna which had an article about a teenage girl pilot. For a year I begged my parents to let me learn to fly. "She'll get over it," they said. When I didn't they took me to a nearby airport for a flying lesson. I was terrified. The airplane was noisy and the instructor yelled. One time he yelled, "RIGHT RUDDER! RIGHT RUDDER!" I kept pushing the right rudder. Finally he realized I was doing that and apologized. After about 6 weeks he moved to the Eastern Shore of Maryland and my mother drove me and my nephews to another airport. (My mother had to babysit her grandchildren a lot.)

This instructor was much nicer. He showed me that the airplane could fly itself—that there was nothing to be afraid of. He taught me all of the basics—right and left turns, climbs and descents, slow flight, stalls, steep turns, a little instrument flying, takeoffs and landings. Finally I made my first solo flight. My mother had cataracts and couldn't see it but some boys told her I had done well. After that the instructor took me on cross country flights. After that I went on solo cross country flights which I really enjoyed. It was such a feeling of freedom to not have my instructor there. Once I got lost and landed at an airport and asked for directions. They told me to follow a major highway and I would find the airport. I passed my private pilot's test. I didn't know what to work on next. Renting an airplane is expensive. I was advised to work on getting a commercial license which was easier then than it is now. What helped me the most was practicing the maneuvers solo—pylon 8's, chandelles, lazy 8's. I also went on many solo cross country flights. My flying felt natural to me after so much solo practice. It felt as natural as driving a car.

Flying helped my self confidence since I was the only teenager in college or high school who could do it but I still didn't have the self confidence others had. We were given a test in freshman year of college which showed I had the lowest self esteem of anyone there. One of the questions was "Do you think you look as good as everyone else?' I answered, "No." I think I deliberately answered some of the questions in a negative way in order to get help (which I wasn't given). I was given a talking to after that.

Although flying didn't improve my self esteem much it did make me less afraid when something untoward happened such as an emergency situation. Once I learned my job, for example, job "emergencies" didn't seem so fearful. You face some dangerous situations flying an airplane. A job emergency is not such a big deal.

One time I flew to Hagerstown, Maryland to get my radio fixed. When I was getting ready to go back I was told that the wind had picked up in Baltimore. They said, "Don't worry. It will be okay." I wasn't worried and they never would have said that to a man. I had read how to land in a crosswind. I landed the way the article said. It was not the way I had been taught. After making a perfect landing I found out it had been a 40 knot crosswind and everyone there had gathered to watch me crash.

One time I traveled on an airliner. It was rocking back and forth, gently. When I disembarked the pilot said, "Sorry for the turbulence, ma'am." Someone said I should have said, "That's nothing compared to landing a Cessna 150 in a 40 knot crosswind." After learning to fly in all conditions most turbulence affecting an airline doesn't bother me.

9. Age 14-17

The high school years were the worst of my life. My mother went from being kind and understanding to being a harridan. The first time she verbally abused me was when she was helping me get ready for a dance. She gave me an antique ring and a blouse that she said was silk. When I told her I had told the other girls that I was going to wear a silk blouse, she screamed, "No one can afford a silk blouse. They will know you were lying." I had merely told them what she had told me.

Another problem was that she didn't notice that I needed a bra at age 13. I was embarrassed by my bosoms. I knew men were looking at them partly because they were unconfined by a bra. My cousin finally looked at me and said, "You need a bra." I told my mother and instead of making this a nice mother-daughter moment and taking me to shop for a bra, she asked my cousin for her old bra. At least it was a bra but my cousin was bigger around the middle so it didn't fit very well. I didn't get a bra that fit until age 17 when I was in my older cousin's wedding.

When I was 17 some girls fixed me up with a boy to take me to the prom. My mother borrowed my cousin's dress which wasn't a perfect fit. My cousin was big at this time. As before, this could have been a good mother daughter moment shopping for a dress for the prom.

I went to an all girls high school so I wasn't exposed to

boys until I learned how to fly at age 17. There were a few that worked at the airport. With no exposure to boys and wanting to do fairly well in school I spent all my weekends studying. It was a difficult school because every Monday they would give us 3 tests. I didn't pay attention during class or take good notes. I fell asleep during class in the morning so I missed a lot of what the teacher said. The only teacher who emphasized things was a history teacher. She'd tell us about historical books and repeat their names loudly and distinctly: HOW THE OTHER HALF LIVES, HOW THE OTHER HALF LIVES. UP FROM SLAVERY, UP FROM SLAVERY. She'd give her opinion also. "Lindbergh should not have been persecuted for saying the Jews caused the war." Beyond that I don't remember much. But I did read *How the Other Half Lives* and *Up From Slavery* as background for my book on Theodore Roosevelt. He was influenced by both of those books and became friends with the authors. She also mentioned a general whose name had a certain "ring" to it. I have forgotten it now but that general moved down the street from my mother. After the war he became a politician and even ran for governor.

My mother would scream at me because I spent too much time in my room studying. She couldn't understand it because in high school she had gone to dances every weekend and become very popular. She had the kind of brain that could remember a chapter by reading it just once. I had to read the chapter, diagram it, then read about the subject in the World Book Encyclopedia. I studied all day Saturday and reviewed the material all day Sunday. To my surprise I was

73

considered to be one of the smartest in my class.

Every time I went in the bathroom, she thought I was masturbating, which I wasn't. She'd yell, "WHAT ARE YOU DOING IN THERE." The first time she barged in. After that I locked the door. She'd yell, "WHY DID YOU LOCK THE DOOR. WHAT ARE YOU DOING IN THERE." I had no clue why she was doing this. One time I was in the downstairs bathroom for a long time splashing water on my face and combing my hair. When I came out she she said, "Daddy had diarrhea and you were hogging his bathroom." (He didn't have diarrhea.)

Back then not many people got their hair styled. I got mine styled once a year. Since my hair was straight and lay flat I should have had it styled more often. My mother never told me I needed to take frequent baths now that I was a teenager so I smelled. Most people can't smell themselves and teenagers are the most smelly. So my hair was not in fashion, I smelled and I looked depressed. The high school girls talked about me behind my back making me even sadder than I already was. I noticed this while walking behind two girls who were talking about me. One said, "She is right behind us." The other said, "That would be terrible." She said, "No really. She is right behind us." Their code name for me was "BJ" since my initials were "MBJ."

A couple of good things happened at this time. My father took me to see former president Eisenhower and his brother Milton at the dedication of Greater Baltimore Medical Center. He took us to Hershey,

74

Pennsylvania to see the room where Jonas Salk announced he had found a vaccine for polio. Our senior class went to New York and the girls taught me how to wash and curl my hair. Since I liked a boy who worked at the airport I washed my hair much more often and stopped biting my nails. These were what people called the *nice* girls. The girls who picked on me the most were known as the *mean* girls.

Once I became infatuated with the boy at the airport and stopped biting my nails my mother began to accept me.

College was easy compared to high school. There was no more studying for a test every Monday. I would stay up all night studying for the quarterly exams. I had learned how to take good notes at that time. I felt sorry for one girl who had to work and who fell asleep during class. The subjects were easy except for philosophy. I had no idea of what the teachers were getting at. I got a D in one class because I attempted to take the oral exam. I should have taken the written one.

I majored in Elementary Education. I was told in senior year that I was much too timid to be a teacher. I did student teaching and a male teacher told me I could never be a teacher. I didn't have the skills. I began to cry. What was I supposed to do for a living?

10. Programming

I worked as an underpaid clerk typist for three-and-a-half years. I resented the low pay because I had a college education and thought I should be making more money. I wasn't making enough to move in with a roommate, get my own apartment or buy a small airplane.

A friend heard me complaining about this and helped me get into a computer programming trainee class. Computer programming was like nothing I had ever done before. I was very bad at it. My coworkers called me stupid. It was easy to write the programs. Most of them had been written by the systems analysts. But the programs were buggy. I made friends with the resident genius. He taught me how to debug programs. Most of the work I did after that concerned debugging.

My best job was at a business in suburban Maryland near where my nephew lived. Early on they tested me to see if I could debug a program. By that time I found debugging programs to be enjoyable. You tracked the bug down in the same way a detective would solve a crime. Then you fixed it. The debugging was important to the company. I usually had to debug a program that had to be rerun. I felt that it was important to the health of the company.

Later we began to write programs. We had classes on how to write programs using the new data base. Everyone would be given an assignment to write a

program.   Everyone else would waste a week
socializing but I would begin writing it right away. I
also would consult with the analyst in an attempt to
understand the purpose of the program. No one else
wanted that background information.

From computer programing I learned how to think
logically and organize my work. This was very helpful
when I began to research and write books on subjects I
was interested in.

These are some of the books I wrote using the skills I
learned in high school, college and at that job.

I had a sincere interest in investigating each subject:

> The War Against Polio
> The Joy of Life: A Biography of Theodore
> Roosevelt
> Manic Depression and Depression: What
> Works
> Better Than Before: How Polio Transformed
> My Father
> Grace to the Humble: Recovering From
> Physical and Mental Illness
> Abraham Lincoln: The Formative Years 1809-
> 1841
> Abraham Lincoln: Ascent to Power 1840-1860
> Preserve Protect and Defend: The Presidency
> of Abraham Lincoln

I worked at that company for five years. By then many
of us felt overworked. We worked a lot of unpaid

overtime. They wanted us to work at night if possible.
Many of us did but we didn't accomplish as much as we
would have during an 8 hour day. Finally my husband
and I moved to Florida so I could escape the pressure.

I got a job at the Space Center in Florida. For two
years it was very low-key. Then I was asked to lead a
young group of programmers.   I was tasked with
teaching them what I knew about the data base,
programming and debugging. At this time my husband,
who had never been happy in our marriage, pretended
he was going to commit suicide. He described in the
detail the methods he was trying.   The talk of suicide
made me so nervous that I flew to see my mother, took
some tours of Delaware landmarks, went to Ocean City
and visited my brother. When I came back I had to
watch my husband, who worked where I did, become
friendly with another woman who he eventually
married.   Between that and some unreasonable
deadlines, it was too much.

That's when I became manic and thought I'd be
reincarnated if I crashed into a tree which I described
before..

11. Depression

My psychiatrist advised me to go back to work after Christmas. I decided to go back in January.

After he stopped the Haldol I felt relaxed for a few days, then I became depressed. My mother was still with me, trying to structure my day for me. We would watch *Eight is Enough* in the morning, then go out to eat at our usual outdoor restaurant, then go to the ocean, then she would fix dinner. Of course she enjoyed these activities also.

She was beginning to worry about her bills. My sister was supposed to be paying them but she hated paying bills. She was an artist and it was totally unnatural for her to keep track of bills or balance a checkbook. She hated it.. She must have had a certain personality known as "scattered." She had been able to make beautiful drawings since the age of 8. You can't help your personality type.   I had another friend who also must be "scattered." She was a hairdresser who was always misplacing her hair implements saying, "Where is it. Where did it go?" She would talk to herself most of the time.

I learned how to draw after taking a class at the age of eleven. I can draw and paint so I must have some talent. It was unfortunate that my sister didn't develop her talent more. But a husband and children kept her too busy.

While my mother was worrying about her bills I had clinical depression. Clinical depression was the worst thing that ever happened to me. Hitting a tree and having some critical injuries was nothing compared to that. I was afraid all the time. I was afraid to answer the phone. I was afraid not to answer the phone. I was afraid to go out. I was afraid not to go out. I was unable to read. I was unable to enjoy watching television. Sleep was not much of an escape. I would wake up at 5 a.m. although I didn't want to. I would wait until 7:30 and then wake my mother. I wished I was dead but didn't have the energy to kill myself.

The psychiatrist told me to stop seeing my ex-husband because it was "confusing me." He talked about getting my mother to leave. Had he seduced me when I was seeing my ex-husband I would have told him. However I did tell two friends. One said not to see him again. Another told me to report him. I immediately started seeing another psychiatrist. She said, "I wonder why your last doctor never gave you antidepressants." When I told her that he seduced me she spun around in her chair and drank a glass of water. She helped me report his behavior to the local mental health authorities but they couldn't believe a doctor would do such a thing. Then she helped me find a lawyer. He probably had doubts about my story but when he went to see the doctor he had hired 5 lawyers. He believed me then. Why hire 5 lawyers if you're innocent? But he said the doctor was very believable.   I was very angry because he didn't give me the antidepressant medication I needed. I am over it now because I've heard he is old and sickly. When someone has one foot in the grave I find it easier to forgive them.

80

When I went back to work I was still in a depression. I probably had brain damage from the accident I had had. Or perhaps my IQ had become lower. I was one of the few laid off from work after the Challenger accident. The layoffs occurred in 1987. As soon as I was laid off I went to Human Resources and told them that my boss was prejudiced against me because I was going to a psychiatrist. After a little investigation, they got me my job back. But not long after that, my boss called a meeting and asked each programmer to document any mistakes I made.

Programmers make mistakes all the time. They spend most of their day correcting them. But H.R. doesn't know this and would take seriously any list of mistakes I made.

I started doing things on my own. I went to Weight Watchers and lost 10 pounds. I took a painting class and began to paint respectable watercolors. We had bought a sail boat so I took sailing lessons. I went to group therapy.

In March of 1988 my boss decided to transfer me. He said that everyone agreed that I was slow and made mistakes. He wanted me to go to a non-programming group. I told him everyone makes mistakes and are not punished for it. Programming was the only thing I knew how to do.

81

"You would be better off out of here," he said.

That evening I meditated on it. My boss was right, I decided. I might end up working for a much nicer person.

The next day, I was transferred—to a small programming group. Under a little pressure by the new boss, I relearned how to quickly solve problems. It was a group of 5 very nice guys who would not have been upset if I had told them I had bipolar disorder. (Which I didn't. The first time I said that it caused quite a bit of shock.)

12. Dr. Cross

Dr. Cross tried several medications which doped me up too much. They were antipsychotics. Finally she tried a tricyclic antidepressant. She knew if this worked it would be because it put me into a slight mania. It did. I felt good but not manic. Then she proceeded to give me my diagnosis:

"You are manic depressive."

"No. My moods are within the normal range."

"Great writers, presidents and poets have it. It is attached to the gene that goes with intelligence. That's why the better families have it."

Because of this I became proud of having manic depression.

Before I got over the depression I met a girl 7 years older than me. She took me out on the weekends. If she couldn't do that she found someone else to babysit me. Being alone is unbearable for a person with depression.

13. My Second Husband

Her friend introduced me to a handsome man. His best feature was his head. He had great hair and his face was good looking. I liked how he dressed. He dressed like the socialites I used to know. He looked classy. He said he had a Honda but on our first date he drove a white Corvette. It was obvious he was showing off. Then he took me to his mother's house. She had Italian tiles in her hallway. I thought that was showing off also. Then he showed me a big painting of his mother when she was younger and said it was painted by the same person who painted Queen Elizabeth. (Many people have painted Queen Elizabeth.) I heard that she didn't like the picture so they put it in a museum. Then he showed me a portrait of his younger brother when he was a toddler. Next he took me to his brother's houses. His brother owned two houses. One was used as a guest house. The main house was beautifully (and expensively) decorated.

However he himself didn't have a job and lived with his mother. His mother wanted to marry him off to me because I was pretty and made a good salary. Eventually I got him a job and we got married.. Then we bought a very inexpensive house but it was clean and recently painted. It had two bathrooms and two bedrooms.

After about 6 months he quit his job because he didn't feel his yearly evaluation was fair. He was rated average instead of above average.

I had been putting up with a lot of verbal abuse for the entire time I knew him. One time we were eating at a buffet and I went up to get my food. I also got a roll. "Where's my roll. Bring me a roll," he said. I didn't. This was before I knew how verbally abusive he could be. He gave me the silent treatment all the way home. At home he said he was going to leave because I was not a very loving person. I begged him to stay. I was remembering how sick I got when my first husband left.

I should not have hung on to him. I made good money. I could easily have left and found myself an apartment. Him leaving would not have hurt me since he was not my best friend as my first husband had been.

Once he quit his job I became very angry. I had been putting up with all the verbal abuse and he leaves his job! That anger is what killed our marriage. He felt it and began to look for another woman.

I was also angry at his mother. She was very wealthy. She lived in a nice house in a good neighborhood. Towards the end she complained I should be feeding her son better so he wouldn't have to go out to breakfast with her. Also I should buy him some new clothes. I, on the other hand, thought wealthy as she was she should be helping to support her son. *Grrr.* It's hard even now to forgive her for not helping me financially. Her mother lived to be 99 so she may still be alive and healthy. I know it's wrong but I still can't forgive her.

My second husband acted like a beautiful woman who

expects someone to take care of her.

The marriage ended when he began to stay away for 5 nights out of the week, probably with another woman. He made it clear to me that he was going to divorce me. I didn't care. I fell in love with my third husband at work and asked my second husband to leave. Not what he expected at all. He was supposed to leave first. He moved into an apartment in the basement of his mother's house. I understand that she finally grew tired of him and he moved into his brother's house.

*****

In 1995 my job became much more complex and I no longer had the ability to do it. I could have handled it years ago but after I had my breakdown it was harder to learn that type of thing. My psychiatrist, Dr. Gonzales, (Dr. Cross had retired to Canada), advised me to go on disability. I was becoming so nervous at work that I was taking too many Klonopin. The type of work I was expected to do required certain abilities that had escaped me during my nervous breakdown.

Because of Dr. Gonzalez I was able to get 2 years of disability from my company. We used that money to buy a better house. It is bigger than our old house, has more bedrooms and is in a better neighborhood. We felt like we were living in a mansion.   I wanted to get Social Security Disability also.   That would provide me with payments until I was 65. It would continue after that as Social Security.

The first judge turned me down because I was too active. I drove a motorcycle, volunteered at the hospital and flew an airplane. (Really my husband flew the airplane. I had lost so much self confidence after my breakdown that I was afraid to fly one.) My lawyer had Dr. Gonzalez give a deposition and also interviewed some of my co-workers at the hospital. The second judge wanted to know how long I sleep. I told him 14 hours. "I've heard enough," he said. "You are disabled."

Don't Tell Anyone Anything
Unbelievable Even if it's True

In 1989 I attended a water color class. They had the radio on. It said there had been an earthquake in San Francisco damaging the Bay Bridge. I went home and said, "There was an earthquake in San Francisco." My husband said, "That's impossible. I was just talking to my sister" (who lives there). I said, "When did you talk to her?" "An hour ago." I told him it occurred after he had spoken to her. I told him to turn on the TV, "any channel." He did and saw that I was right. I had broken the rule that an old journalist had made. "Don't tell anybody anything unbelievable even if it's true."

When Lincoln's Secretary of War, Stanton, was told that Secretary of State Seward had been assassinated, he said, "That's impossible. I saw him an hour ago." The Secretary of State was badly wounded but didn't die. Stanton checked with the messenger to find out more details. Then he hurried to Seward's house. On the way there he heard of Lincoln's assassination. Hoping this wasn't true he headed to Ford's Theatre. Discovering that Lincoln was dying, he placed guards on the cabinet members houses. Eventually he gathered them together and sent a telegram to break the news to the American people.

The other night I told someone that Trump hadn't made up the term "HILLARY FOR PRISON." The Republicans invented that phrase. I saw it when I attended a Republican luncheon and thought it was mean. The speaker that day thought it was funny. Trump said, "LOCK HER UP! LOCK HER UP!" At the next meeting I went to we were asked to raise our hand if we would support Trump if he was nominated. I was the only one who didn't raise their hand. When he was nominated I stopped going to those meetings.

I guess that person thought it was unbelievable that nice Republican ladies would have a picture of Hillary behind bars.

Another Unbelievable Thing

Father Charles A. Arminjon published *The End of the Present World and the Mysteries of the Future Life* in 1881. The book disappeared until one copy was discovered by an American. St. Thérèse had praised the book so the writer felt a calling to translate it into English. It was published in 2008.

The book was well sourced. Only a minimum if it quotes Revelations which many people say is an allegory.

Besides Revelations the sources are:

89

Romans
Monsignor Pichenot, Archbishop of Chambery
Schelling, *Philosophe de la Revelation*
Matthew
Malachi
Luke
Acts
Thessalonians
St. Jerome, Doctor who Translated the Bible into Latin
St. Bede, English monk, scholar, and Doctor
Cornelius a Lapide, *Commentary on Matthew*
Psalms
Isaiah
John
Peter
Daniel
St. Vincent Ferrer, Dominican mission
Preacher who helped to mend the Great Schism of the
West
Second Letter of Ageruchia to Monogamia
St. Cyprian, Bishop of Milan and Martyr
St. Ambrose, Bishop of Milan and Doctor
Philippians

The book has chapters on the signs that will precede the
end of the world, the persecution by the Antichrist and
the conversion of the Jews, the resurrection of the dead,
the glorified body, purgatory, hell, the vision of god, the
means of redemption and suffering. I was impressed
most by the signs that will precede the end of the world
and the resurrection of the dead and the glorified body..

*****

When I'm manic my husband notices it right away and informs me of it. Then we call my doctor to get an antipsychotic which brings me down right away. Once we couldn't get ahold of her so he drove me to her office where I announced that I was manic. The girls in the office acted as if I had said, "I'm having a heart attack." The doctor took me right away and gave me some antipsychotics which she said were very strong. "Go to bed at 9 P.M. and don't drive." I haven't had any more manias since then because I take a little of that antipsychotic.

Lincoln

Children should spend time learning, but should learn what they enjoy. As a boy Lincoln read everything he could get his hands on. He also preached to the other children, mimicking what he heard at church or speaking against cruelty to animals. He was also very compassionate as a child.

At age 22 he moved to New Salem. He read newspapers, history, poetry, prose, philosophy, Shakespeare and grammar. He paid particular attention to the early history of this country. This would help him later in his speeches against slavery. He said the Founders did not think that slavery would continue and some were against it.

By 1833 he decided to study law and surveying. Surveying would bring him in contact with more people. He would be elected to 4 terms in the state legislature. He pushed to move the state capital to Springfield.

He served a term in Congress but he was a failure at that. He was forced to return to his law practice. Knowing that he had mental health problems he worked on them at this time particularly trying to eliminate his flaws.

Since he had worked with an unhelpful lawyer, he became compassionate to young lawyers and gave them lots of help.

He was drawn back into politics by the Dred Scott decision and the Kansas-Nebraska Act, both of which voided most of the Missouri Compromise of 1820. Lincoln feared that when or if the United States acquired Puerto Rico, Cuba, Mexico or part of South America that slaves would be taken there. Also, the Dred Scott decision of 1857 would allow slaves to be taken into free territories, perhaps even into free states. Slavery threatened to spread everywhere and Lincoln felt compelled to stop it.

An anti-Nebraska movement arose and Lincoln took notes about history, the Founders, government and Stephen A. Douglas.

In September of 1854 Lincoln began to give speeches in favor of the Missouri Compromise. He spent much time in the State library studying Congressional speeches and American history and wrote several editorials. He gave a speech in Peoria that contained all of his ideas about slavery. The ideas would remain unchanged until he wrote the Emancipation Proclamation. His subject was the repeal off the Missouri Compromise and the propriety of its restoration.

The Republican Party was organized on Washington's birthday, 1856.

After the anti-Nebraska Act Lincoln was a changed man—more passionate, his speeches more compelling

The Illinois Republicans held a convention on June 16,

1858. Lincoln was chosen as their candidate for the United States Senate. He gave the famous "House Divided" speech where he said, "I believe this government cannot endure, permanently half slave and half free."

He ran against Stephen Douglas. He said, "Let us discard all this quibbling about this man and the other man, this race and that race and the other race being inferior, and therefore they must be placed in an inferior position. Let us discard all these things, and unite as one people throughout this land, until we shall once more stand up declaring that all men are created equal."

He lost because the Illinois legislature, which chose the senator, was mostly Democrat.

He was invited to give a speech in New York. He prepared for this speech more than any other. He used the State library and studied political history. He was trying to prove that the Founders were against slavery and had expected it to end. After he wrote the speech he walked the streets of Springfield saying it aloud. The speech displayed great historical and legal knowledge. He was asked to give that speech in several Northern states. This was the speech that made him famous enough to become president of the United States.

Psychological Health

Most people aren't like Lincoln. They don't want to learn everything about every subject. But everyone can feel a calling to perform some act even if it is just a volunteer job. I felt called to volunteer for the local hospice after my mother died. I was struck by their care of her. I also stayed with her the entire time she was dying so thought I would be good at it. Now I feel I should spend more time writing my books. They are independently published so few people buy them but I learn a lot from writing them and maybe that is their purpose.

Anyone who is mentally ill should find some project to work on. It will take your mind off your problems. If you are not on disability or retired work hard at any job you're given. What you learn from that will come in handy later. Anyone who has bipolar disorder is more likely to be more creative than the average person and even more likely to have a mystical experience.

www.ingramcontent.com/pod-product-compliance
Lightning Source LLC
Chambersburg PA
CBHW070139260726
48658CB00001B/499